MW00901375

HOW TO SUB-2

Subject-To Real Estate Investing Quick-Guide

KIMBERLY BANKS

Copyright © 2021 Kimberly Banks

DEDICATION

For my sons, Robbie and Ben, with thanks for always cheering me on!

CONTENTS

1 INTRODUCTION TO SUBJECT-TO

As I begin this book in what is hopefully the end of the crazy Covid-19 Crisis, and the end of 2020, I am reflecting on the burden this crisis has placed on people the world over, both personally, and financially.

One thing's for sure, you can't bank on your job or even your own business, depending on what it is, to sustain you. There are no guarantees. Having a side-hustle in real estate investing will bring you some income and security, even when your job does not.

I'm not one of those gurus with fancy jets and millions of dollars worth of commercial property, and that's exactly my point.

I want to reach everyday people like me. Anyone can do this. I have flipped lots of properties in ten different states, but that's no big deal compared to the three houses I'm going to tell you about that I bought Sub-2.

As I mentioned, I'm not a huge rental property owner with hundreds of doors. I'm just your every day small investor. In fact, I sold one of the houses I bought Sub-2, and still own the other two, as of this writing. I am always looking to buy new properties, and may well own more by the time this is published. I regret ever selling the rentals and residential properties that I have owned and sold in the past. I have learned it is best to always hang on to your properties.

There may be times when you feel tired of them, but as the mortgages get paid down and rents go up, you'll do well to take my advice and don't ever sell them.

In this book, I will explain what I mean by "Sub-2," how you can buy your first rental property Sub-2 without spending a dime, and I will take you step-by-step through the process I used to acquire these particular three properties.

Dig in, and enjoy!

Question: So, what the heck is Sub-2, Anyway?

Answer: The definition of Sub-2 is as follows:

SUBJECT TO:

"A seller transfers the deed to the property subject to the existing debt staying in place and remaining in seller's name."

In other words, you buy a house without money, and simply take over the owner's mortgage payments. Sound good? It should!

Question: How does it work?

Answer: The key in doing a successful Sub-2 deal begins with finding a super motivated seller, because not just any seller will agree to this plan. Those who really need to get rid of their homes due to some sort of stress, will be your likely candidates for a Sub-2 deal.

When I do a Sub-2 deal, I buy the house for the balance of what is owed on the mortgage. So the purchase price is the balance of what's owed, even if it's under market value.

The key question I ask sellers is, "will you consider selling for the balance of what you owe on it?"

If they say yes, then its time to talk to them about buying their house Sub-2, or "subject to the existing mortgage."

Note:
Please note, while we're on the subject of purchase price, when filling out a contract for a Sub-2 deal, you will use a regular Purchase and Sale Agreement from the state where the property is located, and in the "special stipulations" section, write:

- Buyer purchasing property "Subject To" the existing loan.
- Buyer will make payments on the current loan(s).
- Property will be deeded to Buyer by Seller with a Warranty Deed at closing.
- The total loan amount is approximately $_____.

For the purchase price section, don't put a price, instead write "loan balance at closing," as you do not have this exact number, and your title company or attorney will take care of getting that number just prior to closing.

You also want to specify that the seller pays all closing costs. This way, you are really buying the house for nothing! All you are doing is taking over the mortgage payments, and getting the seller out from under his or her debt.

Q: <u>Is this a loan assumption?</u>

A: No, it is not. When you do a formal loan assumption, you have to qualify with the bank and fill out lots of paperwork, and then the loan gets put into your name.

With a Sub-2 deal, the loan stays in the seller's name. You do not ask the bank' permission at all. You simply begin making the regular monthly payments after closing.

So, the steps to a Sub-2 deal are:

1.   Locate a motivated seller whose house is NOT listed with a real estate agent.

2.   Find out if they are willing to sell for the balance of what's owed on the property.

3. If yes, write up a standard Purchase and Sale Agreement from your state with the "special stipulations" paragraph mentioned above) and have all parties sign.

4. Send the signed agreement to either the title company or real estate attorney.

5. Let the title company or real estate attorney guide you through until closing.

6. Begin making payments on the seller's loan and install tenants in the property.

7. Start marketing for your next Sub-2. Repeat the process.

2 THE PRINEVILLE, OREGON PROPERTY

I heard a great saying a few months ago, and that was simply "don't cut down the cherry tree."

I love this saying so much for both its simplicity and its lesson, and I have vowed to follow it from here on out.

It simply means that if you are lucky enough to own a rental property that produces fruit (cash) for you each and every month of the year, year after year, for God's sake, don't ever sell it!

Don't chop down that cherry tree, that unfailingly gives you fruit, month after month, year after year! I sold this house, and should have kept it!

When I bought my first Sub-2 deal, I was running a nationwide Google AdWords campaign, stating that I buy houses. This is my favorite way to find motivated sellers.

Set up a website saying that you buy houses, set up an ad on Google AdWords that takes sellers to your website, run the ad, and wait for the calls to come in.

If you do not have the money to run a Google ad campaign, then you will have to market in other ways, such as posting daily on Craigslist, writing Yellow Letters, or driving around looking for properties that look vacant (driving for dollars.)

Marketing is really the key. You must do marketing, otherwise you are dead in the water.

I got a call one day from a woman in Prineville, Oregon. I was living in Charlotte at the time, and had never been to Oregon (still haven't), but this did not matter.

I was able to buy her house WITH NO MONEY WHATSOEVER and install a tenant WHO MADE THE PAYMENTS to me and then I paid the seller's mortgage.

What does that equal? A free house! Yes. You read that right. Now read it again!

Nancy (name changed) was definitely a motivated seller. Her husband had lost his job.

"Are you current on payments?" I asked, as I always do.

She said no, but explained that they would not be able make next month's payment, so they were in a real hurry to sell.

It's to your advantage if they are current on their payments, because guess who would have to bring the loan current, if you bought it when the seller was behind? That's right, you would. And the goal here is to buy rental houses with no money.

I asked the sellers if they just wanted to get out from under the debt to avoid foreclosure, and they said yes.

I told them I could take over the payments, and that the loan would stay in place, in their names. They agreed to this, because they were in a situation where they just needed the house gone, like yesterday.

A lot of investors will tell you not to buy a home with little equity, however, I disagree with that. If you can buy a house (for free!) and have your tenant pay your mortgage, that to me is an awesome deal, even if it doesn't have equity when you acquire it, because over the years, the mortgage balance goes down and rents go up (it's a beautiful thing!)

This is not a get rich quick game. It takes time, patience, and perseverance, but it's so worth it in the long run.

I wrote up the contract and emailed it to the sellers through my SignEasy app. They signed and returned it, and then I googled "title companies Prineville Oregon," found one, and emailed the signed contract to the title company. Then we just waited for the title to be pulled and the closing documents to be written up. The title company overnight mailed the docs for me to sign, and the sellers went to the title company to sign them in person, since they lived nearby. And that was that.

Question: How do you handle the insurance on a Sub-2 deal?

Answer: Remember, only an owner can insure a property, so I advise my sellers to have their insurance agent cancel their policy the day after closing.

I, the new owner, start my new policy on the day of closing.

Here are your instructions:

Ordering Insurance for Sub-2 Deals:

1. Owner needs to cancel current policy as of day after closing

2. Request a non-owner occupied "landlord" policy with Kimberly J. Banks (buyer's name) as first named insured

3. Lender is named as mortgagee

4. Prior owner is named as additional insured

Don't worry if the above doesn't make sense to you right now. Give the above information to your insurance agent, and let him or her write the policy.

Next I googled "house cleaners" and had the place thoroughly cleaned after the sellers moved out. The cleaners emailed me photos and it was spotless!

I then posted an ad on Craigslist listing the house for rent.

I ended up finding a young guy with a high credit score, 800 something, who was moving to Prineville. He didn't have a job, but he had a great income from an inheritance, and he sent me the statements to prove it.

I cannot emphasize enough, only take people with high credit scores who do not smoke.

Allow pets. I usually say "up to two friendly pets welcome at no additional charge." I consider pets part of the family, and welcome them to my rentals. I see a lot of landlords advertise "NO PETS," and wonder how they ever get their properties rented!

Question: Is buying Sub-2 legal?

Answer: Yes, of course. I would never do, or advise you to do, anything illegal! There is even a line on the HUD-1 statement specifically for Sub-2.

Question: Do I take title in my name or in a trust, or LLC?

Answer: I bought all of my Sub-2's in my own name, as my motto is always, "keep it simple."

Question: How did you show the property to prospective tenants when you lived in Charlotte and the house was in Oregon?

Answer: I called a locksmith in Prineville who installed a lockbox on the door. I gave the code to people who wanted to look. The code opened the lockbox, and a key was inside.

You can also have the owner hide a key for you before they move out, if you are trying to save money. That works, too.

Have the prospective tenant text you a copy of their driver's license, if you're worried about them harming the property.

Question: How do you actually make the monthly mortgage payments?

Answer: I get the bank log-in details from the seller. Then I can always look up the loan, and they can too, to make sure the loan is being paid. I set up regular payments to the mortgage company in my bill pay. I keep a separate account for each rental.

Make sure your tenants are paying more than what you owe each month. Then it's a good idea for you to pay extra on your payment each month. This will save you interest, and speed up the time until you have paid off the loan completely, and are the proud owner of a cash-flowing free and clear house!

Also, you obviously cannot change the name on the loan online, it must stay in the seller's name, but you can change the mailing address, so that any correspondence the lender sends out reaches you. As my address, I put c/o Kim Banks and my address. When I get mail from the lender, it is addressed to the seller, in care of me.

Some magical things can happen along the way. If there is PMI on the house, it gets dropped when you have built up sufficient equity to satisfy the lender. What does that mean? Your monthly payment gets lower! Magical!

3 CUTE TOWNHOME IN CHARLESTON, WEST VIRGINIA

Again, this is not an area I was familiar with, and had never visited before. Didn't matter. Google is my friend and can tell me all I need to know.

This was a young couple who was recently married. They were living in the townhome that the wife owned prior to the marriage. It was getting to feel too small for them. They were thinking of starting a family.

They had bought another house before selling the townhome, and got stuck with making two mortgage payments every month when the townhome didn't sell. Not fun. Even if you can do it, who would want to? Again, they did not have a lot of equity in the house.

They also had two loans on the property, one small, one big. The small one was used to make the downpayment.

In hindsight, I should have required that they pay off the small loan prior to closing, but I didn't think of it then. I took both loans.

Oh well. It's been five years, and the small loan is paid off now (magical!) After a week or two of trying to decide if they would let me buy the house and take over the mortgage, the wife emailed me to say they would like to move forward with it, because they really did not want to make two payments every month. The townhome had been listed for a few months, and had not sold. By the way, we did not talk on the phone at all. The whole deal was done by email.

So again, I contacted a title company there, BesTitle in Charleston, and sent them the documents once all parties had signed.

<u>Question</u>: How do you get photos / know what the inside looks like if you do not see the property before closing?

<u>Answer</u>: Have the seller take photos of inside and out and email them to you.

<u>Question</u>: Close with an attorney or a title company?

Answer: It depends on the state. You can google it! It seems like out west they mostly use title companies and east coast uses attorneys, but it depends, so do your research.

If you haven't done any real estate deals before, don't worry. Once you have the contract signed by the sellers and you, (you always sign last!), just email the signed contract to the title company or attorney and let them guide you through the process all the way through closing.

I usually specify on the contract a closing date 30 days from the date of signing. That usually gives the attorney or title company ample time to do their thing.

Question: What are some things that might come up prior to closing?

<u>Answer</u>: Liens are a possibility. With the Oregon property that I bought, there was a spousal support lien that the sellers either did not know about or neglected to tell me about. This is why you do not try to do these without the help of an attorney or title company.

Liens are not necessarily a deal killer, and can always be negotiated. I ended up negotiating and paying the spousal support lien so we could close.

All liens need to be taken care of (either paid or released by the lien holder) prior to closing, except of course, the mortgage lien, when doing a Sub-2. That lien stays on place.

4 THE GEORGIA HOUSE

I was advertising in and around Savannah, where I have lived for most of the past twenty years, that I buy houses.

I had an ad on Craigslist that a young woman saw. She called me, and there was almost a desperation in her voice. She really needed my help.

A wholesaler had kept her hanging for a couple of months, saying he would buy her property, but then couldn't find anyone to flip it to, so he got out of the contract.

By the time she called me, she had just about had it with the house and that wholesaler.

I said I could take over the payments immediately, and she was very relieved. As soon as we hung up, I wrote up the Purchase and Sale Agreement, and sent it to her via SignEasy.

She signed and returned the paperwork within the hour.

This young woman was living in North Carolina, and had "friends" as tenants in her old Hinesville house in Georgia, where she used to live, who trashed the place. She was livid and, to boot, had lost her job. This was all too much for her.

She was super nice and easy to work with. Very easy deal all around.

I always keep in touch with the people whose houses I have bought Sub-2, in case I ever need them for anything or they need me for anything.

Then we proceeded to closing and I began to search for a tenant. Seeing a pattern here?

When explaining Sub-2 to sellers, I usually describe it like this - kind of a weird way, but it seems to be understandable.

"Say you have this really rich great aunt. So one year for Christmas, she says, 'Guess what? I'm going to make your house payments for a year. Merry Christmas!' She writes a check to the bank every month. The bank is happy. You are happy.

Does the bank care that the name on the check does not match the name on the loan? Hell no, as long as they get their money, and get it on time!"

And that brings me to another point: you absolutely, positively MUST make that payment, whether your tenant pays you or not. If you EVER get into a situation in which you are unable to make that payment, you MUST give the property back to the seller!!! If you promise to make payments on someone's mortgage and then you don't, that's fraud. And fraud can put you in jail. Enough said.

You have a big responsibility when it comes to taking a property Sub-2.

You are now responsible for someone else's credit. Your good payments will help their credit. Being late with payments or, god forbid, missing a payment, will damage their credit.

So do your best to honor the seller's credit and your promise to them.

Question: What happens if I stop making payments on a house I bought Sub-2?

Answer: The bank takes the house back (forecloses) and THE SELLER'S CREDIT TANKS! And you could be in a lot of trouble.

I know you will never, ever let that happen!

Question: What's the ideal scenario for a Sub-2?

Answer: The ideal scenario for the seller is that at some point you refinance the home into your name, if you want to keep it. That would be ideal.

Question: How will I be able to talk to the bank about a loan that is not in my name?

Answer: Get the seller to sign an "Authorization to Release Information" form prior to closing.

This tells the bank that the borrow agrees to let you speak to the bank about the loan.

Most banks have this form available for download on their website.

Tips for Screening Tenants

I use Zillow to screen my tenants.

Question: What does Zillow cost?

Answer: As of this writing, Zillow is free for landlords. Prospective tenants pay an application and screening fee. I do everything through Zillow, from listing the property to screening tenants to collecting rent payments. Zillow does it all! I love it.

Make sure the tenants have verifiable monthly income of at least 3x the monthly rent.

Make sure they have great credit! You can put this in your ad:

The minimum rental requirements are:
1. No criminal or eviction record
2. Credit score is 680 and better
3. Income is at least 3 times the rent

Question: How do you deal with repairs on the property, if you do not live in the city where the rental is located?

<u>Answer</u>: My tenant sent me a text one morning when I was teaching. It said that the hot water tank was spewing water everywhere.

Yikes. Not a good text to get first thing in the morning, but you just have to put your big girl (or boy) pants on, and deal with it. Problems do not happen often at all, but when an issue does arise, deal with it, and solve the problem right away.

My tenant made a quick call to the water department to tell them to turn off the water, while I called a plumber. Problem solved quickly.

<u>Question</u>: What happens if you have to evict a tenant?

<u>Answer</u>: The only times I have had to evict tenants were when I did not screen well. Remember that!

If you get good tenants with good credit, you will likely not have to evict them.

Be strict about who you let in there, because you will be dealing with them for at least a year, and maybe ten! I have one tenant who is going on her fourth year. (She's great.) If you do have to evict, get online, and google "evictions [county where property is located]."

You will probably end up at the website of the magistrate court, which will give you step-by-step instructions.

You can do this yourself, or you can hire a lawyer. Just make sure you follow the process. It will be spelled out on the website and you can do most of it online. I really recommend buying rentals in landlord-friendly states. You can find these by googling "landlord-friendly states." Buying rentls in landlord-friendly states will make your life as a landlord a lot easier.

Owning rental property can be so rewarding. You can go from a net worth of zilch to a net worth of _____ insert any number, depending on the number of properties you acquire.

And you can do it at no cost to you!

These properties can be handed down to your kids free and clear one day, giving them income every single month, which is far better than leaving them a big lump sum.

I hope I have piqued your interest in buying properties Sub-2, and given you some great tips on how to go about it.

The attorney Bill Bronchick, has an excellent and reasonably-priced course on Sub-2 investing. You might want to check it out. You can google it!

Make sure you start telling people you buy houses.

Wear a button that says you buy houses.

Get the word out.

Start posting it everywhere, online and in stores.

Get cheap business cards at VistaPrint, and get rolling.

You need to get the phone ringing and talk to lots of sellers. If you do not like to talk to sellers, do not worry. Text them! You got this!

Do not get frustrated if people say no to you. It will take time for you to build confidence when talking to sellers and it will take time for you to find sellers who are truly motivated. A truly motivated seller NEEDS TO SELL, as opposed to WANTS TO SELL. Big difference. After a bunch of no's, one day you may just get a yes, and that yes will change your life!

Question: Can I live in one of the houses I buy Sub-2?

Answer: Yes, of course you may.

Question: What do I say when a seller calls me?

<u>Answer</u>: Ask these questions:

Can you tell me about the house? (Let them talk and take notes!)
Why are you selling it?
What repairs does it need?
How much is still owed on the house?
Would you sell for the balance of what's owed?

Try to sprinkle the questions into the conversation, as opposed to making it sound like an interview. Listen to what they need and try to help them.

If they say yes to "would you sell for the balance of what's owed?," this is a potential Sub-2 deal! Yay!

Please note: if they own the house free and clear, they cannot do a Sub-2 on it, because there is no mortgage to take over. In this case, maybe they will sell it to you on monthly payments, though!

This is called seller financing, and is also a great strategy to acquire properties. Seller financing is also great when they say no to "will you sell for the balance of what's owed?"

There is an old saying in real estate, "your price, my terms" or "my price, your terms."

Remember, an investor can buy in one of two ways: <u>for cash</u> or <u>on terms</u>, either:

• deeply discounted for cash

(in which case we assign the contract to a landlord or house flipper who has cash, if we don't - known as wholesaling)

Or

- close to full market value on terms

- (monthly payments, as mentioned above, or Sub-2)

When you ask the sellers why they are selling, there are certain words to listen for, which indicate motivation.

Remember, non-motivated sellers will not sell you their house Sub-2. Listen for words like divorce, illness, job transfer, death in the family, need to sell fast, etc., which indicate motivation and a NEED TO SELL.

Question: What is the "due on sale" clause?

Answer: Most all loans today have a clause which allows the lender to call the loan due upon transfer of title. This is called the "due on sale" clause.

You need to make the seller aware of this clause, in full disclosure, but in all my years of investing and in all real estate groups, I have rarely seen this happen, unless the payments were not being made. Keep the payments current - pay well before the due dates, and pay more than what's due, and the bank should stay very happy.

If for any unknown reason the loan is called due, you can always reach out to the bank to negotiate this. First guy says no? Find his supervisor.

Your other options, of course would be to sell or refinance the property. Generally speaking, you likely won't have to deal with this issue. Banks have the right to call the loan due, but that doesn't mean they ever will have reason to. Don't give them a reason.

I am afraid I have to wrap it up here, but I thank you so much for reading my book. I really appreciate it, and really hope that I have dropped some golden nuggets that will help you in your real estate investing career or side hustle! If you have found value in this book, could you please do me a favor, and leave me a review on Amazon? I would so appreciate it!

Thank you so much and good luck. There is so much I want to tell you about other strategies when a Sub-2 won't work. Maybe in the next book?

I love teaching and learning about real estate.

Cheers!
Kim

ABOUT THE AUTHOR

Kimberly Banks has been buying houses in Savannah, Georgia, and nationwide since 2006. She bought her first rental house at auction on the steps of the Chatham County Courthouse, and has been hooked on real estate ever since. Kim has been a real estate agent, landlord, investor, and homeowner. Originally from Connecticut, she lives in Savannah and has two grown sons.

Made in the USA
Columbia, SC
29 December 2023

29664858R00028